Thank you for purchasing this coloring b
If you enjoyed it and want more pages in
on Amazon and email me at ivytintswor
You'll receive 10 additional printable co
hours.

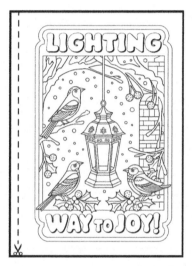

This Book Belongs To

This Book Belongs To

Test Color Page

Bright and Merry Days

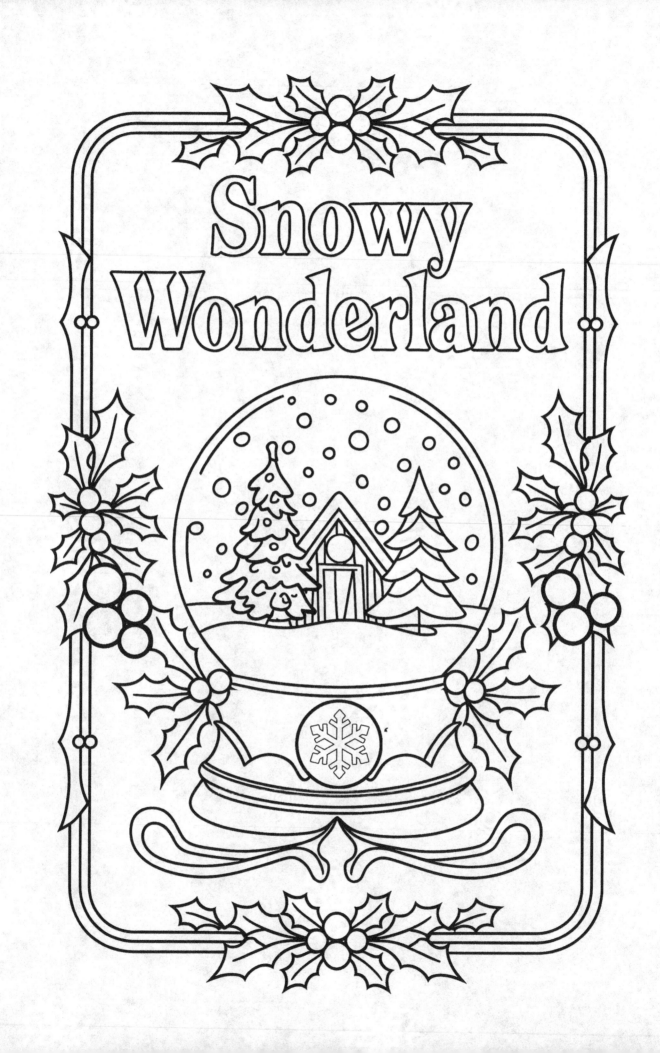

FROSTY
FUN

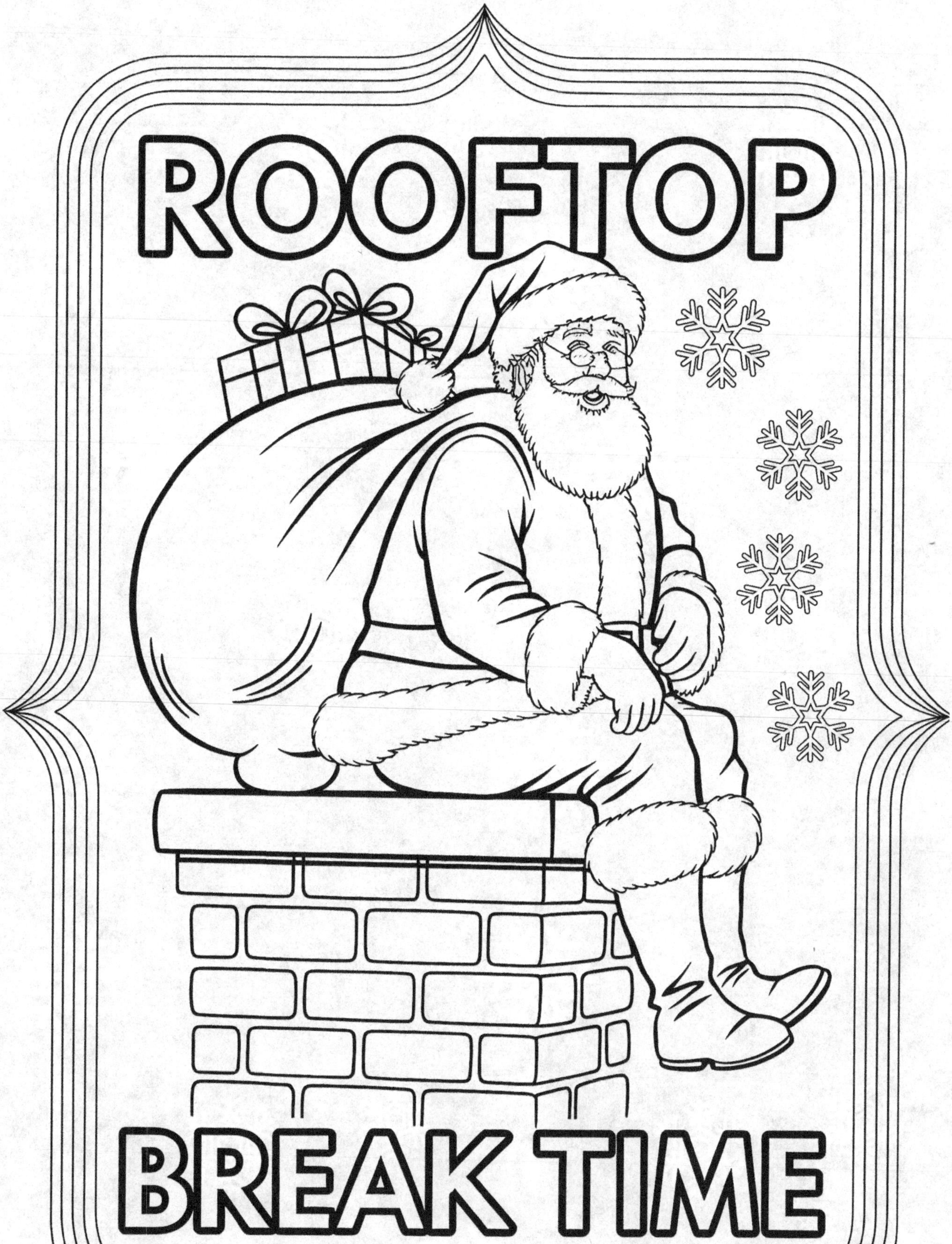
ROOFTOP
BREAK TIME

HOPING FOR A PRESENT

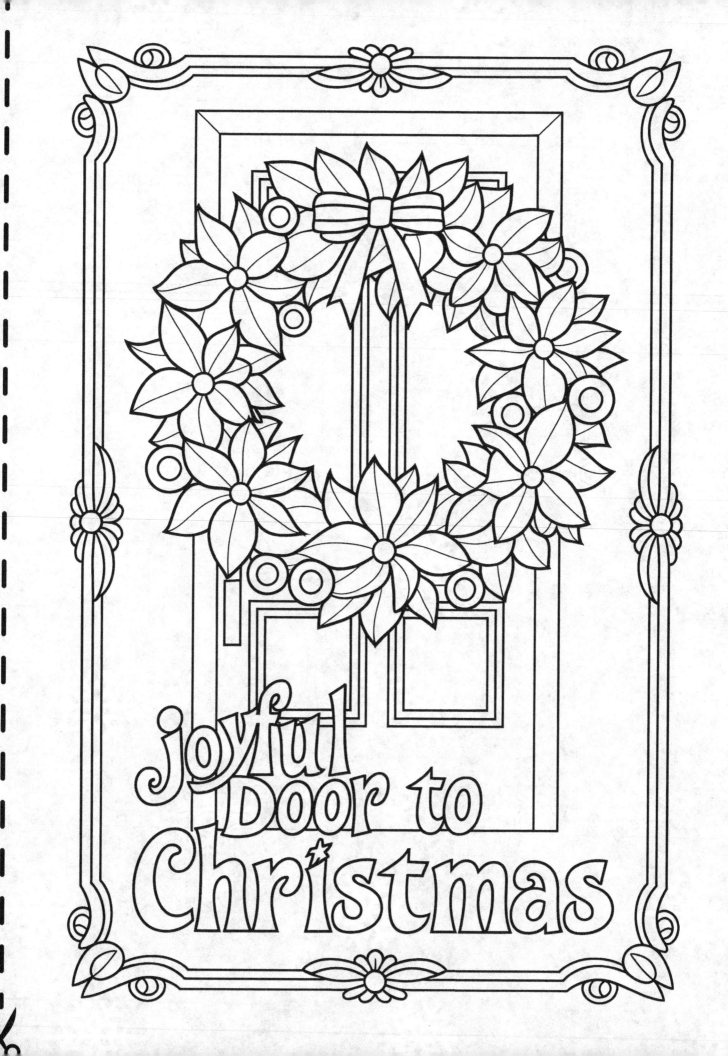

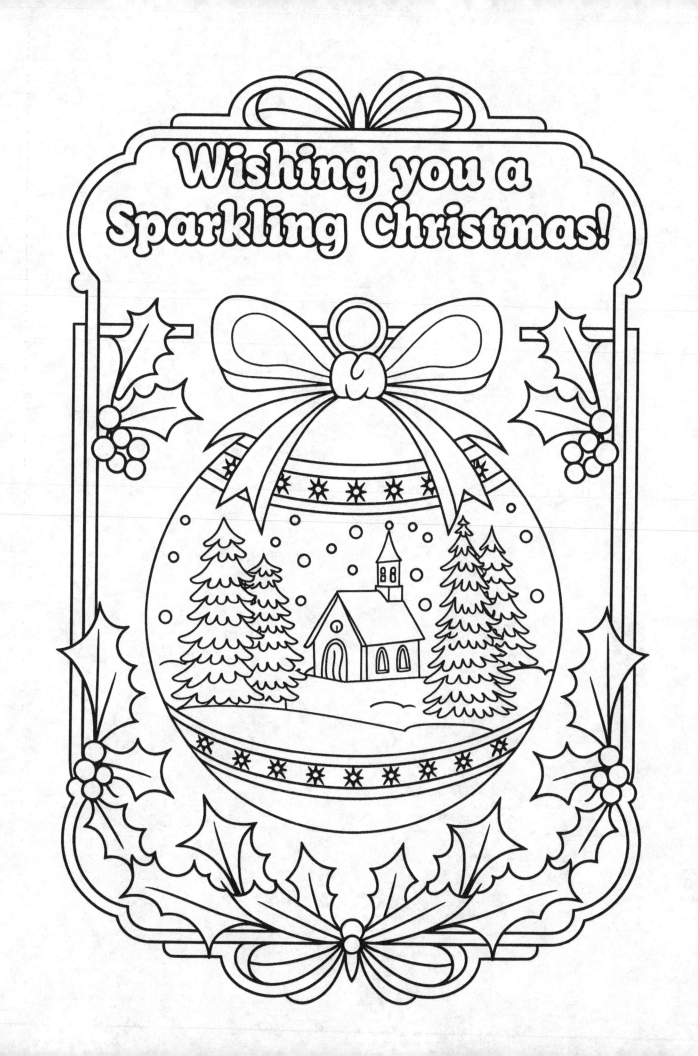

COUNTDOWN TO CHRISTMAS

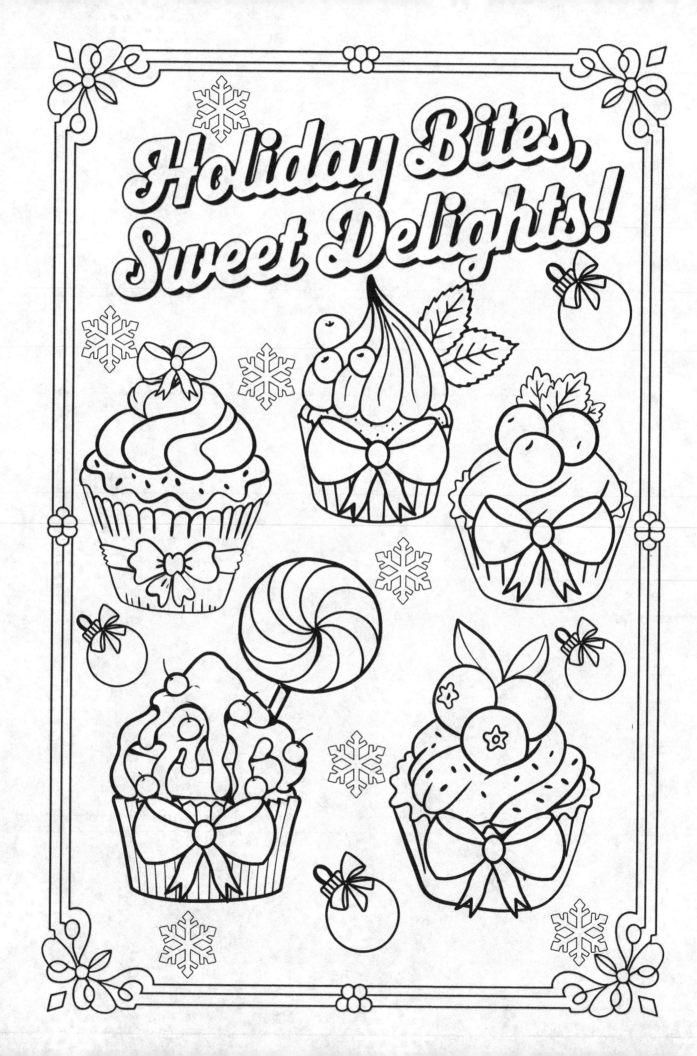

Merry Christmas and Happy Coloring

Ivy Tintsworth

Made in the USA
Monee, IL
25 October 2024

68675000R00057